Drawing and Learning About Faces

Using Shapes and Lines

by
Amy Bailey Muehlenhardt

Thanks to our advisers for their expertise, research, and advice:

Barbara Schulz, Comic Book Illustrator
Adjunct Faculty, Design
Minneapolis College of Art and Design, Minneapolis, Minnesota

Susan Kesselring, M.A., Literacy Educator
Rosemount-Apple Valley-Eagan (Minnesota) School District

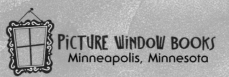

PICTURE WINDOW BOOKS
Minneapolis, Minnesota

Amy Bailey Muehlenhardt
grew up in Fergus Falls, Minnesota,
and attended Minnesota State
University in Moorhead. She holds
a Bachelor of Science degree in
Graphic Design and Art Education.
Before coming to Picture Window
Books, Amy was an elementary art
teacher. She always impressed upon
her students that "everyone is an artist."
Amy lives in Mankato, Minnesota,
with her husband, Brad.

To Brad—each day I'm with you,
I become more of myself. I love you!
To my Waconia students—every time you solve
a problem, you are thinking like an artist.
Be creative, and keep drawing!

ABM

Managing Editor: Bob Temple
Creative Director: Terri Foley
Editor: Sara E. Hoffmann
Editorial Adviser: Andrea Cascardi
Designer: Amy Bailey Muehlenhardt
Page production: Picture Window Books
The illustrations in this book were drawn with pencil.

Picture Window Books
5115 Excelsior Boulevard
Suite 232
Minneapolis, MN 55416
1-877-845-8392
www.picturewindowbooks.com

Printed in the United States of America.

Library of Congress Cataloging-in-Publication Data
Muehlenhardt, Amy Bailey, 1974-
Drawing and learning about faces : using shapes and lines /
by Amy Bailey Muehlenhardt.
p. cm.— (Sketch it!)
Summary: Provides instructions for using simple shapes
and lines to draw faces.
Includes bibliographical references.
ISBN 1-4048-0271-1 (Reinforced Library Binding)
1. Face in art—Juvenile literature.
2. Drawing—Technique—Juvenile literature.
[1. Face in art. 2. Drawing—Technique.]
I. Title: Faces. II. Title.
NC770 .M84 2004
743.4'2—dc22
2003019284

Table of Contents

Everyone Is an Artist
There is no right or wrong way to draw!

With a little patience and some practice, anyone can learn to draw. Did you know every picture begins as a simple shape? If you can draw shapes, you can draw anything.

The Basics of Drawing

line—a long mark made by a pen, a pencil, or another tool

guideline—a line used to help you draw. The guideline will be erased when your drawing is almost complete.

shade—to color in with your pencil

value—the lightness or darkness of an object

shape—the form or outline of an object or figure

diagonal—a shape or line that leans to the side

Before you begin, you will need:

a pencil
an eraser
lots of paper

Four Tips for Drawing

1. Draw very lightly.
To see how this is done, try drawing soft, medium, and dark lines. The softer you press, the lighter the lines will be.

2. Draw your shapes.
Connect them with a dark, sketchy line.

3. Add details.
Details are small things that make a good picture even better.

4. Smudge your art.
Use your finger to rub your lines. This will soften your picture and add shadows.

Let's get started!

Simple shapes help you draw.

Practice drawing these shapes before you begin:

 **circle**
A circle is round like a bouncing ball.

 **triangle**
A triangle has three sides and three corners.

oval
An oval is a circle with its cheeks sucked in.

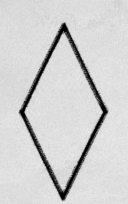 **diamond**
A diamond is two triangles put together.

 **arc**
An arc is half of a circle. It looks like a turtle's shell.

square
A square has four equal sides and four corners.

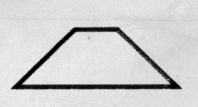 **trapezoid**
A trapezoid has four sides and four corners. Two of its sides are different lengths.

 **crescent**
A crescent looks like a banana.

 **rectangle**
A rectangle has two long sides, two short sides, and four corners.

You will also use lines when drawing.

Practice drawing these lines:

vertical

A vertical line stands tall like a tree.

horizontal

A horizontal line lies down and takes a nap.

diagonal

A diagonal line leans to the side.

dizzy

A dizzy line spins around and around.

zig zag

A zig-zag line is sharp and pointy.

wavy

A wavy line moves up and down like a roller coaster.

Remember to practice drawing.

While using this book, you may want to stop drawing at step five or six. That's great! Everyone is at a different drawing level.

Don't worry if your picture isn't perfect. The important thing is to have fun. You may wish to add details to your drawing. Is the happy person at a party? Did the scared person see something frightening? Create a background.

Be creative!

7

Happy

When you feel happy, your eyes are bright. Your mouth opens wide with a great big smile. If your friend comes over to play or you get a good grade in school, you probably have a happy face.

Step 1

Draw an oval for the head. Draw two guidelines. One of your guidelines should be horizontal, and the other should be vertical.

Step 2

On the horizontal guideline, draw two large ovals for eyes. Draw two small ovals for the pupils. Draw two short, diagonal lines for the eyebrows.

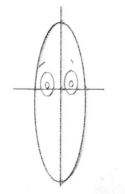

Step 3

On the vertical line, draw a zig-zag line for the nose. Draw two curved lines for the wide, open mouth.

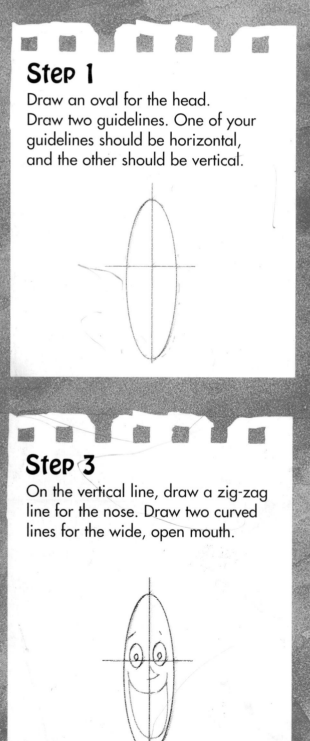

Step 4

Draw two curved lines for the upper and lower teeth. Add a heart-shaped tongue.

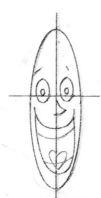

Step 5

Draw two arcs for ears. Add squiggly lines inside of the ears. Use zig-zag and wavy lines for the hair.

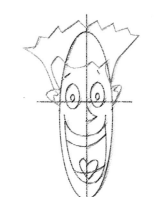

Step 6

Trace over the lines you want to keep. Add curved lines on the face for cheeks. Erase the guidelines and other lines you don't need.

Step 7

Draw two vertical lines for the neck. Shade in the hair, eyes, and mouth. Shade between the two front teeth to make a gap.

Embarrassed

When you are embarrassed, your cheeks turn red. Your eyes grow large and round. When you walk into the wrong classroom by mistake or get called on by the teacher and forget the answer, you probably have an embarrassed face.

Step 1

Draw an oval for the head. Draw two guidelines. One of your guidelines should be horizontal, and the other should be vertical.

Step 2

On the horizontal guideline, draw two large ovals for eyes. Add two smaller ovals for the pupils.

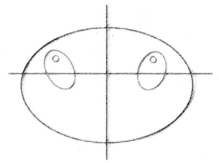

Step 3

Draw two wavy lines for eyebrows. On the vertical guideline, draw a curved line for the nose.

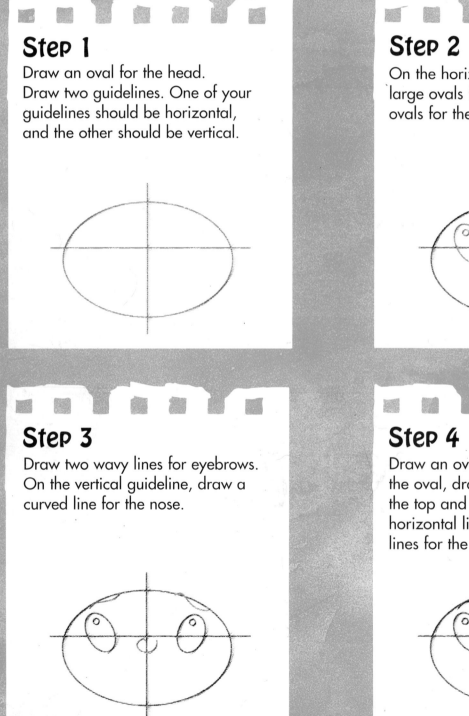

Step 4

Draw an oval for the mouth. Inside the oval, draw two curved lines for the top and bottom lip. Draw a horizontal line and short vertical lines for the teeth.

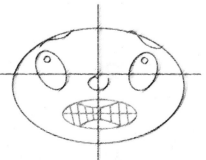

Step 5

Draw two arcs for the ears. Add squiggly lines inside of the ears. Draw wavy lines for curly hair.

Step 6

Continue adding wavy lines for hair. Trace over the lines you want to keep. Erase the guidelines and other lines you don't need.

Step 7

Add two vertical lines for the neck. Add curved lines below the eyes for cheeks. Shade in the cheeks with your pencil. Shade in the hair, eyes, and eyebrows.

Angry

When you are angry, your eyes narrow sharply. Your face looks pinched. If the neighbor kid breaks your favorite toy or your sister won't get out of your room, you probably have an angry face.

Step 1

Draw an oval for the head. Draw two guidelines. One of your guidelines should be horizontal, and the other should be vertical.

Step 2

On the horizontal guideline, draw two ovals for eyes. Add two small circles for the pupils.

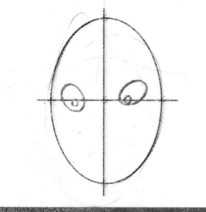

Step 3

Draw a diagonal line on top of both ovals. Draw two wavy lines for eyebrows. The eyebrows should be tilted downward.

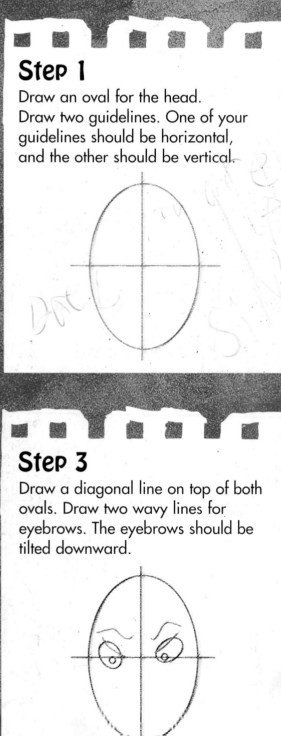

Step 4

On the vertical guideline, draw a curved line for the nose. Draw a wavy line for the frown. Draw two arcs for the ears. Add squiggly lines inside the ears.

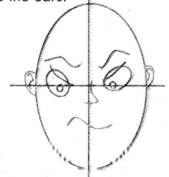

Step 5

Draw a lot of wavy lines for the hair.

Step 6

Continue adding wavy lines for hair. Trace over the lines you want to keep. Erase the guidelines and other lines you don't need.

Step 7

Erase the tops of the oval eyes. Add two vertical lines for the neck. Continue shading in the hair, eyes, and eyebrows. He has dark, curly hair.

Surprised

When you are surprised, your eyes grow wide. Your mouth is shaped like the letter O. When someone sneaks up behind you or tells you something amazing, you probably have a surprised face.

Step 1

Draw an oval for the head. Draw two guidelines. One of your guidelines should be horizontal, and the other should be vertical.

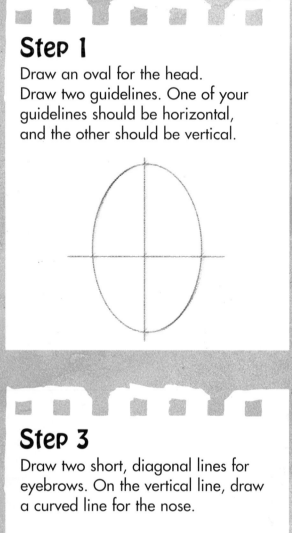

Step 2

On the horizontal line, draw two large ovals for eyes. In the middle of the eyes, draw two small ovals for pupils.

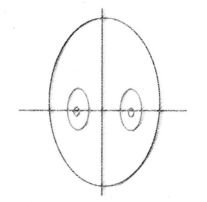

Step 3

Draw two short, diagonal lines for eyebrows. On the vertical line, draw a curved line for the nose.

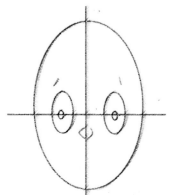

Step 4

On the vertical line, draw a small oval for the surprised mouth. Draw two arcs for the ears. Add squiggly lines inside of the ears.

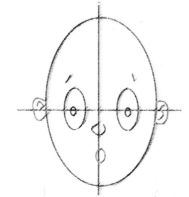

Step 5

Draw long, wavy lines for hair.
Add more wavy lines for pigtails.

Step 6

Trace over the lines you want
to keep. Erase the guidelines
and other lines you don't need.

Step 7

Add short lines for eyelashes. Add a barrette to her
hair. Shade in the eyes, eyebrows, hair, and mouth.

Excited

When you are excited, your eyes might grow wide. A big smile might appear on your face. If you're going on a fun trip or to a friend's birthday party, you probably have an excited face.

Step 1

Draw an oval for the head. Draw two guidelines. One of your guidelines should be horizontal, and the other should be vertical.

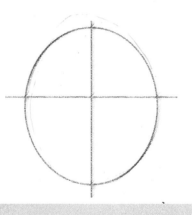

Step 2

Draw two large, oval eyes on the horizontal guideline. Draw two small ovals inside the eyes for pupils. Add two short, curved lines for eyebrows.

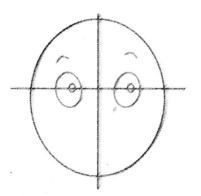

Step 3

On the vertical guideline, draw the letter c for the nose. Draw two curved lines for the smile. The smile should look like an arc.

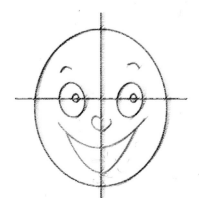

Step 4

Draw two curved lines for the top and bottom teeth. Add small curved lines for the corners of the mouth.

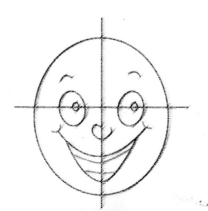

Step 5

On the horizontal guideline, draw two arcs for ears. Add squiggly lines inside the ears. Draw zig-zag lines for hair.

Step 6

Trace over the lines you want to keep. Erase the guidelines and other lines you don't need.

Step 7

Draw two vertical lines for the neck. Use your pencil to shade in the mouth, hair, and eyes.

Sad

When you feel sad, your face looks droopy. Your lower lip quivers and your eyes look down. If your team loses the game or you argue with a friend, you probably have a sad face.

Step 1

Draw an oval for the head. Draw two guidelines. One of your guidelines should be horizontal, and the other should be vertical.

Step 2

Draw two ovals for eyes. Add two small ovals for pupils. Draw two curved lines for eyebrows.

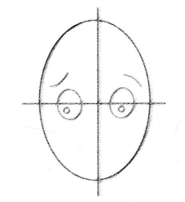

Step 3

On the horizontal guideline, draw a curved line for the nose. It should look like the letter J. Draw a curved line for the mouth and a wavy line for the lower lip.

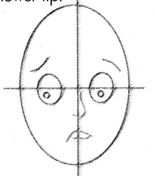

Step 4

Draw two arcs for ears. Add squiggly lines inside the ears. Add ovals with pointed ends for tears.

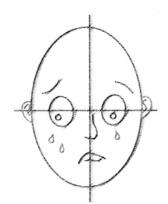

Step 5

Draw long, wavy lines for the hair.

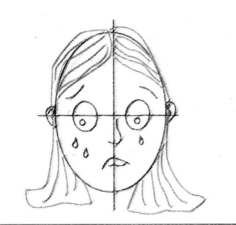

Step 6

Trace over the lines you want to keep. Erase the guidelines and other lines you don't need.

Step 7

Add short lines for eyelashes. Shade in the eyebrows, eyes, and hair with your pencil.

Bratty

When you feel bratty, your eyes grow narrow. You might grin through your teeth. When you talk back to your parents or play a joke on your best friend, you probably have a bratty face.

Step 1

Draw an oval for the head. Draw two guidelines. One of your guidelines should be horizontal, and the other should be vertical.

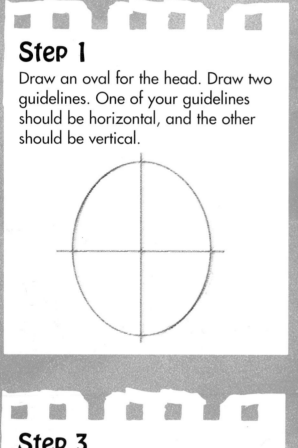

Step 2

On the horizontal guideline, draw two ovals for the eyes. Add two small circles for the pupils.

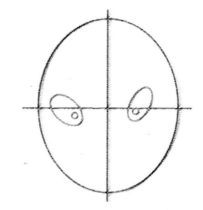

Step 3

Draw two diagonal lines for the eyebrows. On the vertical guideline, draw a curved line for the nose. The nose looks like the letter C.

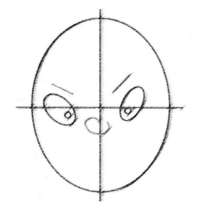

Step 4

Draw two curved lines for the smile. The curved lines touch on one side. Add vertical lines for teeth and curved lines for corners of the mouth.

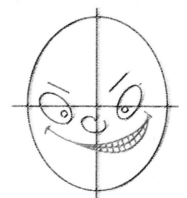

Step 5

Draw two arcs for the ears. Add squiggly lines inside the ears. Use wavy and zig-zag lines for the hair.

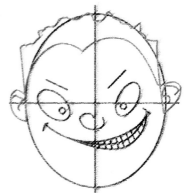

Step 6

Trace over the lines you want to keep. Erase the guidelines and other lines you don't need.

Step 7

Draw two vertical lines for the neck. Shade in the eyes, eyebrows, and hair.

Scared

When you are scared, your mouth turns downward. Your eyebrows are raised with fear. When you listen to a ghost story or hear a bump in the night, you probably have a scared face.

Step 1

Draw an oval for the head. Draw two guidelines. One of your guidelines should be horizontal, and the other should be vertical.

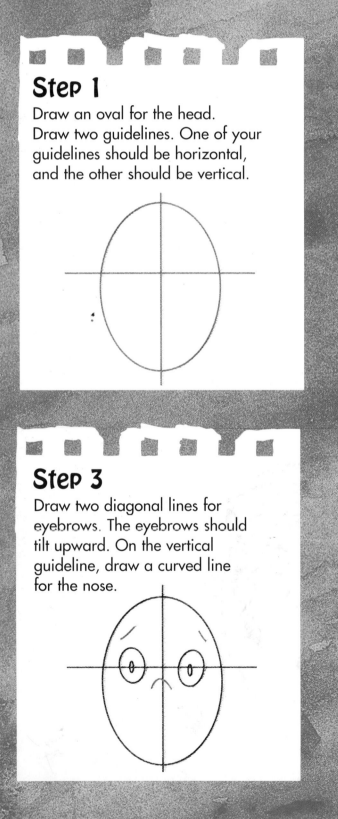

Step 2

On the horizontal guideline, draw two large ovals for eyes. Add two small ovals in the eyes for pupils.

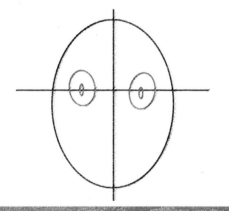

Step 3

Draw two diagonal lines for eyebrows. The eyebrows should tilt upward. On the vertical guideline, draw a curved line for the nose.

Step 4

Draw a rectangle for the mouth. Draw two arcs for ears. Add squiggly lines inside the ears.

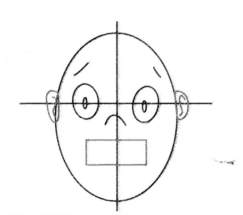

Step 5

Draw dizzy lines for hair. Add wavy lines for the mouth and top row of teeth. Draw the top of a heart for the tongue.

Step 6

Continue adding dizzy lines for hair. Trace over the lines you want to keep. Erase the guidelines and other lines you don't need.

Step 7

Draw two vertical lines for the neck. Continue shading in the hair with dizzy lines. Shade in the mouth, eyes, and eyebrows. Add short, curved lines for eyelashes.

To Learn More

At the Library

Ames, Lee J. *Draw 50 Famous Faces*. Garden City, N.Y.:
Doubleday, 1990.

Baumbusch, Brigitte. *The Many Faces of the Face*. New York:
Stewart, Tabori & Chang, 1999.

Emberley, Ed. *Ed Emberley's Drawing Book of Faces*. Boston:
Little Brown & Co., 1992.

Frost, Helen. *Feeling Happy. Mankato, Minn.*: Pebble Books, 2001.

Hart, Christopher. *Making Funny Faces: Cartooning for Kids
(and Grownups)*. New York: Watson-Guptill Publications, 1992.

On the Web

Fact Hound

Fact Hound offers a safe, fun way to find Web sites related to this book.
All of the sites on Fact Hound have been researched by our staff.
http://www.facthound.com

1. Visit the Fact Hound home page.
2. Enter a search word related to this book,
   or type in this special code: 1404802711.
3. Click on the FETCH IT button.

Your trusty Fact Hound will fetch the best sites for you!